Alfred Görgens

Cooking for
One or Two

Cookery Editor Sonia Allison

Series Editor Wendy Hobson

foulsham

Foreword

Now that supermarkets and other food shops are going in for 'smalls' instead of concentrating mainly on family-size packs, the shopper catering for one or two people has a much greater range of foods from which to choose, making life altogether easier and providing choice without waste plus the opportunity of preparing gourmet meals on a small scale. Loose produce – such as fruit and vegetables – which can be picked over for size, quality and appearance and bought individually are a boon to every small household (after all, who wants a tray of eight potatoes or six tomatoes when two will do). Equally helpful are delicatessen counters nowadays from which one can buy a slice or two of meat, salami, interesting cheese, tasty salads and even a wedge of pizza without recourse to a multi-portion pack.

For solo cooks and pairs, shopping and cooking is much less tedious than it used to be, and with this handsome little book at your elbow, almost anything and everything is possible, whether it's a quickie such as Minute Steak with Banana Curry, a luxury slice of fillet steak in a vegetable and red wine sauce or a downy-like apple snow with raisins. The name of the game is smart, appetising and visually appealing.

Contents

Cooking for One or Two

In this chapter you will find a range of hints and tips on cooking in small quantities which will help you make the best of the recipes that follow.

Pots and Pans

Two saucepans and two frying pans are basically all that is needed when you are cooking for one or two people, but an electrically-heated wok, non-stick for preference, is also a treasure in that food in it can be fried, stir-fried, stewed and simmered without burning and drying out.

If you are searching out new pans for general purposes, broad-based and shallowish pans are a better bet than those with tall sides which often tend to be narrow for ease of use. Pans should have well-fitting lids, preferably with a steam vent.

Aluminium Pans
Aluminium pans are the lightest of all to handle, but make sure they have a heavy base for even heat distribution and maximum efficiency. If the bases are too thin, foods tend to burn. Choose pans with a non-stick coating to prevent direct contact between the food and the aluminium which is now considered to be a health risk.

Cast Iron Pans
These are very similar to copper in use but are very heavy to handle. You should therefore avoid them if you have difficulty lifting heavy pans.

Copper Pans
These come into the all things bright and beautiful category and are much favoured by chefs. For safety, all pans should be lined with tin to prevent acidy foods coming into direct contact with the copper and setting up an unhealthy chemical reaction. But they do gleam regally, especially when highly polished, and do much to enhance kitchen decor.

Enamel Pans
Easy to clean and usually in lovely colours and designs, enamel pans are very heavy and therefore unsuitable for anybody who finds it difficult to lift heavy pans.

Microwaveware
Round, shallowish cookware is best for general cooking purposes and it should be light in colour where possible. This is because some of the darker pottery can absorb excessive amounts of heat, making cooking times longer. Also it can become uncomfortably hot, needing care in handling.

Stainless Steel Pans
These have an extremely long life, but for even distribution and conduction of heat should be heavy-based with, preferably, an inlay of copper. They are expensive but worth the outlay in the long run. They are also fairly light to handle.

The Singles' Pantry

No one wants to be dashing out to the shops all the time, so a well-stocked store cupboard is a real asset in the kitchen. This is the same for a large family as for someone cooking alone or for two people, but it is much harder for those using only small quantities as even food with a long shelf life cannot last for ever.

It is obviously important to be aware of how long particular foods can be stored so that you use all

produce at its best, and certainly before it begins to deteriorate. This includes both basic stock and fresh produce. Basic stock includes foods that can be stored for several months to a year: items such as cereals, dried peas and beans, honey, coffee, rice, dried fruit and so on. Fresh produce, such as milk, cheese, meat, fruit, vegetables and so on, must obviously be stored more carefully and used quickly.

When you shop for stock items, take note of shops where you can buy small packets or can purchase items loose in small quantities. It will not be economical to buy the larger family packs of store cupboard items if you do not use them up, so restrict yourself to larger packets of those goods you know you will use. If, for example, you do a lot of baking, it may be worthwhile to buy a large bag of flour. On the other hand, if you only use it very occasionally, the saving made by buying the larger bag will be lost when you have to throw half of it away after it has lingered in the cupboard past its sell-by-date.

Similarly with fresh foods, shop in places where you can buy just two apples or a few tomatoes rather than in shops where the items are pre-packed in larger quantities. That way you will always use fresh goods at their best.

A little planning goes a long way when you are trying to ensure that your food remains fresh. Try to spend a little time before you go shopping to plan your week's meals. Then you will not fall into the trap of buying more vegetables than you can possibly eat before they go off.

Storing Foods

Food will last longer and taste fresher if it is properly stored, and this brief guide will give you some ideas on the most efficient way to store common foods.

Bread
Bread and rolls can be frozen with minimal loss of taste and texture. This is the easiest way of storing them for more than a few days. If the bread is required quickly, it can be thawed out in a microwave oven for a few minutes, depending on the size. It is better, however, to take a loaf out of the freezer the night before it is needed and let it thaw out overnight.
Store bread in a cool place, in a bread bin or in the bottom of the fridge. The bread bin should be cleaned out regularly with warm water and a dash of vinegar then dried thoroughly. This prevents the growth of mould.

Butter
Keep butter covered in a cool larder or cool spot in the kitchen, or in the refrigerator. If you keep it in the refrigerator, remember to remove it a little while before you need it so that it can soften slightly to make it easier to spread. Butter also freezes well for longer-term storage.

Cheese
Harder types of cheese such as Cheddar, Gouda, Edam and Parmesan can be kept in a suitable cheese box or wrapped in foil in a cool place, not necessarily in the refrigerator.
Soft cheese such as cream cheese, Brie or Camembert should be wrapped in foil and refrigerated. Remove them from the refrigerator at least half an hour before eating so that they can ripen.
Some cheese, such as firm sheep's cheese or Mozzarella must be stored in their own whey or in a bowl of cool salted water in the refrigerator.

Coffee
In an airtight packet, cool and away from the light, ground coffee will keep for at least six months. An opened packet should always be stored in the refrigerator in an airtight container or glass jar to keep its flavour. It is better to buy coffee beans and grind them yourself as they will keep their flavour longer than ready-ground coffee. Instant coffee can be stored in its jar in a cupboard.

Eggs
Eggs should be stored in a cool larder or in the refrigerator. If you have kept eggs for some time and are not sure if they are fresh, you can use a simple test. Gently lower the egg into a bowl of cold water. A stale egg will float to the top and should be thrown away, whereas a fresh egg will sink to the bottom.

Flour
Do not buy flour in larger quantities as it does deteriorate if stored for too long. Keep it in an airtight

container in a dry, cool cupboard away from strong-smelling foods, as it readily picks up aromas.

Fruit
Fruit should be stored in a cool place, either a larder or in the bottom of the refrigerator. Remove fruit from plastic bags before you store it, and avoid the temptation to decorate your room with a large bowl of fresh fruit. It may look good, but the fruit will deteriorate very quickly in a warm room.

Milk
Despite the storage advantages of UHT milk, it really does not taste as good as fresh milk, and you can buy milk in small quantities in most corner shops, or have it delivered daily. Choose whole milk, semi-skimmed or skimmed as you prefer and keep it in the refrigerator. Make sure that you use it in the order in which it was bought so that it is always fresh. It will keep for a few days.

Pasta and Rice
Dried pasta and rice store well in airtight jars or containers in a kitchen cupboard. It is better to buy just one or two types of pasta at a time so that you can be sure of using it up before its sell-by date.

Potatoes
Store potatoes in a perforated vegetable rack or other suitable container away from sun and damp. Another method is to ask your greengrocer for a small wooden crate. Place the potatoes inside and cover with some brown paper to protect them from the light.

Vegetables
Vegetables should be stored in a cool place, either a larder or in the bottom of the refrigerator. Make sure you remove them from plastic bags before storage to discourage them from growing mould.

Using Up Leftovers

When you are cooking for one or two, it is inevitable that you will have leftover foods from time to time. You can often use them up as side dishes to a main course, or add them to a stir-fry or omelette to make a new dish. The recipes in this book also suggest some good ways of using up leftovers.

Another way to avoid having leftovers at all is to cook in larger quantities and freeze some portions for use another day.

Here are a few more ideas.

Cereals and Pulses
These can be added to stews, casseroles and salads, or served separately as a side dish to accompany a main course. Cooked rice can be mixed with some fresh herbs and a little oil and baked inside a hollowed out tomato for a tasty snack. Cooked rice or pasta can be mixed with some chopped peppers, onions and cubes of cooked meat or prawns and dressed with mayonnaise or French dressing to make a wonderful salad.

Fish
Raw fish leftovers make a wonderful stock if simmered gently with a few vegetables and fresh herbs. This can then be strained and frozen for use in fish sauces or soups.

Fruit
Fruits such as melon or even strawberries can be cooked in a risotto for an unusual and delicious dish. You can also use up fruit in trifles or make it into purées, fools or whips.

Meat and Sausages

These cannot be kept for too long, so need to be used while they are fresh. They can be cut into strips and added to fried rice, a noodle dish or fried potatoes with a few chopped vegetables to make an interesting dish. That way, you will need less meat to make a substantial meal. They can also be thinly sliced and used as a sandwich filling or diced and added to soups to make them more of a meal in themselves.

Vegetables

Small piece of leftover vegetables can be added to soups and stews. Larger pieces, such as cauliflower or broccoli florets, can be coated in a white sauce, sprinkled with cheese and baked for a few minutes as a side dish or a complete meal. Whole or halved potatoes are suitable for slicing and frying either on their own or with onions, to be topped with a fried egg for a delicious quick supper. Split jacket potatoes, then mix the potato with egg and grated cheese, top with more grated cheese and grill or bake for a few minutes. Mashed potatoes can be made into croquettes, coated with egg and breadcrumbs and fried.

11

Notes on the Recipes

1 Follow one set of measurements only, do not mix metric and Imperial.

2 Eggs are size 2.

3 Wash fresh produce before preparation.

4 Spoon measurements are level.

5 Adjust seasoning and strongly-flavoured ingredients, such as onions and garlic, to suit your own taste.

6 If you substitute dried for fresh herbs, use only half the amount specified.

7 Preparation times include preparation and cooking and are approximate.

8 Kcals are per portion and are approximate.

9 All recipes serve one unless otherwise indicated. If you are cooking for two, simply double the quantities.

Quantities for Single Meals

Here are a few of the main food items listed in portion-sizes in order to help you to estimate quantities when buying and cooking.

Remember that the recipes list ingredients for one portion, so double them if you are serving two.

Meat, raw weight
Allow 125 to 175 g/4 to 6 oz per serving.

Fish, raw weight
Allow about 200 to 225 g/7 to 8 oz per serving.

Rice and pasta (uncooked)
Allow 50 g/2 oz per serving.

Pulses (uncooked)
Allow 50 g to 75 g/2 to 3 oz peas, beans and lentils for serving.

Potato products, ready-to-cook
Allow 125 to 175 g/4 to 6 oz per serving.

Quick Meals

If you fancy a tasty meal
but are pushed for time,
try some of these
delicious and quick
ideas.

*Piquant Apricot Kebabs
page 16*

Piquant Apricot Kebabs

Preparation time: 10 mins
440 kcal per portion

150 g/**5 oz** lean pork, cubed

2 large mushrooms, halved

juice of ¹/₂ lemon

6 dried apricots

2.5 ml/**¹/₂ tsp** paprika

2.5 ml/**¹/₂ tsp** mixed herbs

salt and white pepper

10 ml/**2 tsp** vegetable oil

1 Sprinkle the pork and mushrooms with lemon juice. Thread them alternately with the apricots on to 2 skewers.
2 Season with paprika, mixed herbs, salt and pepper.
3 Brush with oil and fry for 7 to 9 minutes, turning occasionally until cooked through and golden brown. Serve with crusty French bread or crisp rolls.

Photograph page 14

Pork Steaks with Banana Curry

Preparation time: 5 mins
410 kcal per portion

2 × 100 g/**4 oz** pork steaks

5 ml/**1 tsp** paprika

salt and white pepper

15 ml/**1 tbsp** butter or margarine

a pinch of curry powder

1 small banana, thickly sliced

30 ml/**2 tbsp** soured cream or crème fraîche

1 or 2 slices white or brown toast, freshly made

1 Season the steaks on both sides with paprika, salt and pepper. Heat half the butter or margarine in a frying pan over a medium heat. Add the steaks and fry fairly briskly for 5 minutes, turning twice. Reduce the heat and continue to fry for a further 8 to 10 minutes or until cooked through.
2 Transfer the steaks on to a warmed plate and keep hot.
3 Melt the remaining butter or margarine in the same frying pan, stir in the curry powder and add the banana slices. Stir in the cream or crème fraîche and fry for 1 minute. Turn over the bananas very carefully with a spatula so that they do not disintegrate.
4 Serve the banana curry and the toast with the steaks.

Photograph opposite (top)

Cheese Nut Burger

Preparation time: 10 mins
410 kcal per portion

30 ml/**2 tbsp** finely ground hazelnuts or almonds

30 ml/**2 tbsp** oat flakes

2.5 ml/**¹/₂ tsp** mixed herbs

10 ml/**2 tsp** cream or curd cheese

1 egg, beaten

salt

15 ml/**1 tsp** vegetable oil

10 ml/**2 tsp** plain flour

1 slice wholegrain bread

butter or margarine for spreading

1 green lettuce leaf

1 small tomato, sliced

1 Mix together the hazelnuts or almonds, oat flakes and herbs. Gently whip the cheese and the egg together, season lightly with salt and fold into the hazelnut mixture.
2 Heat the oil over a medium heat in a frying pan. Shape the nut mixture into a burger shape and coat both sides with the flour. Fry the burger until crisp, turning twice.
3 Meanwhile, spread the bread with the butter or margarine and arrange the lettuce on top. Place the burger on top and garnish with the tomato.

Photograph opposite (bottom)

Piquant Cheese Omelette

Preparation time: 10 mins
570 kcal per portion

---

50 g/2 oz soft sheep's or goat's cheese

5 ml/1 tsp chopped fresh herbs (parsley, basil, thyme, chervil)

2.5 ml/1/2 tsp paprika

1 pickled onion, thinly sliced

2 eggs, beaten

10 ml/2 tsp butter or margarine

---

1 Mash the cheese with a fork. Add the herbs, paprika, salt and onion and mix well. Blend the eggs into the cheese mixture.
2 Melt the butter or margarine in an omelette pan. Pour in the egg mixture, cover loosely, and cook for 3 to 4 minutes until the egg miixture thickens and sets and you can lift it up arounnd the edges. Transfer to a plate and eat with bread or toast.

Photograph opposite (top left)

Quick Pan Pizza

Preparation time: 15 mins
530 kcal per portion

---

1 egg

10 ml/2 tsp plain flour

10 ml/2 tsp whipping cream

a pinch of dried oregano

a pinch of white pepper

5 ml/1 tsp butter or margarine

1 small tomato, sliced

2 black or green olives, stoned and sliced

2 slices salami

2 slices Gouda cheese

a few chopped oregano leaves

---

1 Whisk together the egg, flour, cream, a little salt, the oregano and pepper. Dice the cheese.
2 Melt the butter or margarine over a medium heat in a frying pan and pour in the egg mixture. Arrange the tomato slices, olives and salami on top and cover with the cheese.
3 Cover pan and fry the pizza for about 4 minutes until the egg mixture is firm and the cheese has melted. Sprinkle with a little oregano and serve.

Photograph opposite (top right)

Soy Bean Sprouts with Ham Sausage

Preparation time: 15 mins
450 kcal per portion

---

30 ml/2 tbsp vegetable oil

1 small German ham sausage, sliced

1 leek cut into rings

1/2 onion, cut into rings

75 g/3 oz bean sprouts

salt and white pepper

a few drops of tabasco or soy sauce

---

1 Heat the oil in a frying pan over a medium heat.
2 In the meantime cut the ham sausage into slices around 5 mm/1/4 in thick. Clean leek or leeks and wash. Peel the onion. Cut both into thin rings.
3 Add the sausage, leek, onion and bean sprouts to the pan and season to taste with salt, pepper and tabasco or soy sauce. Fry for 5 minutes, stirring frequently. Serve with boiled rice or a slice of toasted rye bread with garlic butter (page 21).

Photograph opposite (bottom)

Cheese and Ham Dream with Onion

Preparation time: 5 mins
390 kcal per portion

5 ml/**1 tsp** butter or margarine
1 slice rye bread
1 slice cooked ham
1 slice Gouda cheese, diced
10 ml/**2 tsp** finely chopped fresh basil or parsley
1 small onion, cut into rings
½ tomato
freshly ground black pepper

1 Melt half the butter or margarine in a frying pan over a medium heat. Spread the remaining butter on the slice of bread and place the ham on top. Transfer the slice of bread to the frying pan, ham side uppermost.
2 Sprinkle with the cheese, cover the pan and cook gently for 1 to 1½ minutes until cheese begins to melt. Sprinkle with the basil or parsley.
3 Transfer the bread out of the frying pan to a warmed plate and keep it hot. Add the onion rings and the tomato to the pan and fry for about 2 minutes.
4 Arrange the onion rings and tomato on the bread and season to taste with a little freshly ground black pepper.

Photograph (top)

Garlic Bread with Stuffed Tomato

Preparation time: 15 mins
190 kcal per portion

1 tomato
15 ml/*1 tbsp* cottage cheese
10 ml/*2 tsp* chopped fresh parsley
1 slice wholewheat bread
1 small clove garlic, crushed
5 ml/*1 tsp* butter or margarine

1 Cut a sliver off the top of the tomato to use as a lid. Scoop out the inside with a spoon and reserve for soup or stews. Mix the cheese with the parsley and spoon into the tomato.
2 Toast the bread. Meanwhile, peel and crush the garlic clove.
3 Mix together the garlic and the butter or margarine and spread on to the warm toast. Top each slice with a filled tomato.

Photograph (bottom)

> **Gourmet Tip**
> To make a larger quantity of garlic butter, mix 100 g /4 oz softened butter with 15 ml/1 tbsp finely chopped fresh parsley, a crushed garlic clove, a little lemon juice and salt. Cover and keep in a refrigerator for up to 3 days.

21

Anchovy Toast

Preparation time: 10 mins
140 kcal per portion

5 ml/1 tsp butter or margarine

½ onion, finely chopped

1 small clove garlic, crushed

1 slice white bread

3-4 anchovy fillets

4 to 5 capers

5 ml/1 tsp chopped fresh parsley

1 Peel the onion and finely chop. Peel the garlic and crush. Melt the butter or margarine over a medium heat in a small frying pan and fry the onion and garlic for a few minutes until soft but not browned.
2 Toast the bread. Spread the onion mixture over the toast and arrange the anchovies and capers on top.
3 Garnish with the parsley to serve. You can add a few strips of olive, if liked.

Photograph opposite (top)

Tasty Tuna Snack

Preparation time: 15 mins
350 kcal per portion

1 slice pumpernickel or other dark bread

butter or margarine for spreading

1 hard-boiled egg, sliced

50 g/2 oz tuna fish, flaked

salt ¼ red pepper, cut into strips

3 black olives, stoned and cut into strips

1 Spread bread thinly with the butter or margarine and arrange the egg on top.
2 Place the tuna around the egg slices and sprinkle with a little salt.
3 Arrange the pepper strips and olives on top.

Photograph opposite (centre)

Gourmet Tip
Any leftover pepper can be used up in the Pork with Paprika Sauce (page 38) or sliced into a salad.

Toasted Cheese with Wine

Preparation time: 15 mins
580 kcal per portion

2 slices white bread

butter or margarine for spreading

45 ml/3 tbsp dry white wine

75 g/3oz Gruyère cheese, grated

1 egg

salt and white pepper

a pinch of ground mace

1 Spread the bread with the butter or margarine and place in a flameproof dish, buttered sides down. Sprinkle with half the wine.
2 Mix the cheese with the remaining wine and the egg. Season to taste with salt, pepper and mace.
3 Spread the cheese mixture over the bread and grill gently until melted but not browned.

Photograph opposite (bottom)

Amsterdam Baguette

Preparation time: 10 mins
490 kcal per portion

---

1 small baguette

butter or margarine for spreading

4 slices pepper salami

10 ml/**2 tsp** mayonnaise

½ onion, cut into rings

1 small tomato, sliced

salt

10 ml/**2 tsp** chopped fresh parsley

2 slices Edam cheese, grated

---

1 Cut the bread open lengthways and spread both halves with butter or margarine. Place 2 slices of salami on each half and spread with a little mayonnaise.
2 Arrange the onion and tomato over the bread halves, then season lightly with salt and sprinkle with parsley.
3 Arrange the cheese on top and grill for about 3 minutes until bubbling.

Photograph opposite (top)

Gourmet Tip
You can vary this recipe in many different ways. Try spreading the baguette halves with herb butter, topping with Camembert cheese and onion rings, then heating under the grill. A filling of boiled ham, pickled gherkins, pineapple pieces and Gouda is equally tasty. For a more piquant sandwich use pepper salami, picked peppers and slices of blue cheese.

Baked Egg with Ham

Preparation time: 15 mins
220 kcal per portion

---

5 ml/**1 tsp** butter or margarine

5 ml/**1 tsp** chopped fresh chives

1 egg

1 slice cooked ham, diced

salt

3-4 green peppercorns

a pinch of paprika

---

1 Well grease a ramekin dish with the butter or margarine and sprinkle the base with chives. Dice the ham.
2 Break the egg carefully into the dish over chives then top gently with the ham and season to taste with salt. Sprinkle over the peppercorns.
3 Cover the dish with foil and stand it in a basin of water. Bake in a preheated oven at 180°C/350°F/ gas mark 4 for about 5 minutes. Remove the foil and bake for a further 5 to 10 minutes until cooked.
4 Using a knife, very carefully run it along the inside of the dish to loosen the egg. Tip it out on to a warmed plate, sprinkle with paprika and eat with a crusty roll.

Photograph opposite (bottom)

Salads

Colourful salads are easy enough to put together at very little expense and are a favourite at home or for the lunch box.

Hazelnut and Vegetable Salad, page 28

Hazelnut and Vegetable Salad

Preparation time: 15 mins
300 kcal per portion

75 g/3 oz lamb's lettuce

1 tomato, cubed

2 thick slices cucumber, peeled and cubed

1 thick slice Gouda cheese, cubed

10 ml/2 tsp coarsely chopped hazelnuts

10 ml/2 tsp balsamic vinegar

salt and freshly ground black pepper

10 ml/2 tsp olive oil

1 Select the best of the lettuce, wash it well, drain and separate into leaves.
2 Mix together the lettuce, tomato, cucumber, cheese and hazelnuts.
3 To make the dressing, mix together the vinegar, salt, pepper and oil and pour over the salad. Toss until well mixed.

Photograph page 26

Lettuce with Banana Sauce

Preparation time: 10 mins
112 kcal per portion

1/2 small lettuce

1/2 banana, sliced

5 ml/1 tsp lemon juice

30 ml/2 tsp natural yoghurt

salt and white pepper

a few mint leaves

1 Tear the lettuce into small pieces.
2 Reserve a few banana slices for garnish. Mash the remainder with the lemon juice and yoghurt and season to taste with salt and pepper.
3 Arrange the lettuce on a plate. Spoon over the banana sauce, top with the reserved banana slices and garnish with mint leaves.

Photograph opposite (top)

Gourmet Tip
You can use soured cream instead of yoghurt. Try it with just a touch of curry powder.

Cress Salad with Smoked Salmon

Preparation time: 15 mins
170 kcal per portion

10 ml/2 tsp lemon juice

10 ml/2 tsp whipping cream

10 ml/2 tsp crème fraîche

5 ml/1 tsp Worcestershire sauce

10 ml/2 tsp finely chopped fresh dill

salt and freshly ground black pepper

1/2 bunch watercress

25 g/1 oz smoked salmon, cut into strips

1 black olive, stoned and finely chopped

1 Whisk the lemon juice with the cream, crème fraîche and Worcestershire sauce. Stir in the dill and salt and pepper to taste.
2 Arrange the cress in a bowl and pour over the sauce. Arrange the strips of salmon on top and garnish with the finely chopped olives.

Photograph opposite (bottom)

Bean and Bacon Salad

Preparation time: 20 mins
670 kcal per portion

200 g/*7 oz* green beans

5 ml/*1 tsp* butter or margarine

50 g/*2 oz* lean bacon, diced

a pinch of dried thyme

a pinch of dried savory

1 small onion, finely chopped

10 ml/*2 tsp* white wine vinegar

a pinch of cayenne pepper

salt

30 ml/*2 tbsp* walnut or olive oil

3-4 walnuts, coarsely chopped

2-3 black olives, stoned

1 Cook the beans in boiling salted water for about 6 minutes. Drain well.
2 Meanwhile, melt the butter or margarine in a frying pan over a medium heat. Add the bacon, thyme and savory then fry until the bacon is crisp.
3 Add the onion and stir well. Add the beans and toss carefully. Spoon into a dish and leave to cool.
4 Mix together the wine vinegar, cayenne pepper and salt and slowly beat in the oil.
5 Pour the dressing over the salad. Sprinkle the walnuts on top and garnish with the olives.

Photograph opposite (top)

Fill-You-Up Salad

Preparation time: 10 mins
530 kcal per portion

50 g/*2 oz* sheep's cheese, cubed

1 slice mortadella sausage or cooked ham, cubed

75 g/*3 oz* lettuce

1 tomato, quartered

1 radish, sliced

5-6 walnuts, coarsely chopped

3-4 green olives, stoned (optional)

10 ml/*2 tsp* white wine vinegar

2.5 ml/*¹/₂ tsp* prepared mustard

30 ml/*2 tbsp* olive oil

5 ml/*1 tsp* chopped fresh tarragon

salt and freshly ground black pepper

1 Toss together cheese, mortadella or ham, lettuce, tomato, radish, walnuts and olives, if using.
2 To make the dressing, mix together the wine vinegar and mustard, then gradually beat in the oil. Season with the tarragon, salt and freshly ground black pepper.
3 Pour the dressing over the salad and toss together gently.

Photograph opposite (bottom)

Avocado Salad with Egg and Salmon

Preparation time: 30 mins
880 kcal per portion

1 ripe avocado

juice of ¹/₂ lemon

1 hard-boiled egg, cubed

10 ml/2 tsp hazelnuts, coarsely chopped

50 g/2 oz smoked salmon, cut into thin strips

10 ml/2 tsp sunflower oil

2.5 ml/¹/₂ tsp Dijon mustard

a pinch of mixed herbs

a pinch of cayenne pepper

5 ml/1 tsp mayonnaise

1 Peel and core the avocado, cut it into 1 cm/¹/₂ in cubes and sprinkle it with half the lemon juice.
2 Mix the avocado with the egg, hazelnuts and salmon.
3 Mix together the remaining lemon juice, the oil, mustard, mixed herbs, cayenne pepper and salt.
4 Pour the dressing over the salad and garnish with the mayonnaise.

> **Gourmet Tip**
> Avocados are ripe when they give a little when pressed with the thumb. Always keep at room temperature as they lose their flavour in the refrigerator. When preparing avocados, the flesh should be sprinkled with a little lemon juice at once to prevent discoloration.

Chicory Salad with Mango

Preparation time: 15 mins
210 kcal per portion

---

1 chicory head

1/2 ripe mango, peeled and cubed

10 ml/2 tsp cider vinegar

a pinch of cayenne pepper

a pinch of salt

10 ml/2 tsp walnut oil

10 ml/2 tsp coarsely chopped walnuts

---

1 Remove the outer leaves of the chicory and cut out the bitter core from the base. Wash the head, drain well and cut into small strips.
2 Mix the chicory carefully with the mango.
3 Mix together the cider vinegar, cayenne pepper, salt and oil. Pour the dressing over the salad, sprinkle the walnuts over the top and toss gently to mix.

Photograph opposite (top)

Gourmet Tip
An alternative dressing for this salad can be made by mixing 10 ml/2 tsp of mango chutney with 10 ml/2 tsp olive oil.

Spinach Salad

Preparation time: 15 mins
270 kcal per portion

---

75 g/3 oz young spinach or dandelion leaves

1 radish, cut into strips

15 ml/1 tbsp cashew nuts

2.5 ml/¹/₂ tsp mild mustard

10 ml/2 tsp herb vinegar

2.5 ml/¹/₂ tsp honey

15 ml/1 tbsp walnut oil

salt and white pepper

a pinch of ground mace or nutmeg

---

1 Wash the dandelion or spinach leaves, drain well and tear into large pieces. Mix with the radish and most of the cashew nuts.
2 Mix together the mustard, herb vinegar and honey then beat in the oil a little at a time. Season the dressing well with salt, white pepper and a touch of ground mace or nutmeg.
3 Carefully toss the salad with the dressing. Finally garnish with a few cashew nuts.

Photograph opposite (centre)

Curly Lettuce Salad with Egg and Nuts

Preparation time: 15 mins
490 kcal per portion

---

1 small head of curly lettuce

50 g/2 oz cured ham, diced

1 hard-boiled egg, diced

3 black olives, stoned and cut into strips

1 small onion, finely chopped

2.5 ml/¹/₂ tsp made mustard

juice of 1 lemon

30ml/2 tbsp olive oil

15 ml/1 tbsp chopped fresh parsley

15 ml/1 tbsp cashew nuts

---

1 Wash and drain the lettuce. Then tear it into pieces and put into a bowl.
2 Mix in the ham, egg, olives and onion.
3 Mix together the mustard and lemon juice and beat in the oil. Stir in the parsley and pour over the salad.
4 Leave the cashew nuts whole or chop coarsely and sprinkle over the top.

Photograph opposite (bottom)

Main Courses

However little time you have and even if you don't feel like going to too much trouble, you can prepare delicious meals on a small scale.

Pork with Paprika Sauce,
page 38

Pork with Paprika Sauce

Preparation time: 30 mins
760 kcal per portion

1 small red pepper, cut into strips
60 ml/4 tbsp dry white wine
150 ml/¹/₄ pt/²/₃ cup double cream
200 g/7 oz fillet of pork
salt and white pepper
a pinch of paprika
5 ml/1 tsp butter or margarine
1 small onion, finely chopped

1 Place the pepper strips, wine and cream in a small saucepan, bring to a simmer and simmer over a medium heat until the mixture is reduced to half its original quantity. Stir occasionally.
2 Cut the pork fillet into 2 cm/1 in thick slices and season both sides with salt, pepper and paprika.
3 Melt the butter or margarine in a frying pan. Briskly fry the pork fillets for 2 minutes, turning twice. Lower the heat, cover the pan and continue to cook for 8 to 10 minutes, again turning twice and adding the onion half way through.

4 Arrange the fillet slices on a warmed plate. Add the wine mixture to pan juices, quickly bring to the boil and pour over the meat. Serve with boiled potatoes or other vegetables of your choice.

Photograph page 36

Pork Steak with Pistachios

Preparation time: 25 mins
490 kcal per portion

5 ml/1 tsp butter or margarine
12 pistachio nuts, shelled and chopped
1 small clove garlic, crushed
a pinch of dried marjoram
1 × 150 g/5 oz pork steak
2.5 ml/¹/₂ tsp honey
a pinch of paprika
salt and white pepper
10 ml/2 tsp olive oil
2 tomatoes, sliced
freshly ground black pepper

1 Melt the butter or margarine in a frying pan over a medium heat. Add the pistachios, garlic and marjoram to the pan and fry for 1 to 2 minutes.
2 Meanwhile, make a 4 to 5 cm/1¹/₂ to 2 in cut in the steak with a sharp knife and spread the inside with honey. Season inside and out with a little salt, white pepper and paprika. Fill the pork steak with the pistachio mixture.
3 Heat the oil in the frying pan over a medium heat and fry the steaks briskly on both sides until sealed. Reduce the heat and continue to fry for 7 to 8 minutes until cooked through.
4 Sprinkle the tomato slices with pepper. As soon as the steak is cooked, transfer it to a warmed serving plate. Fry the tomatoes for a few seconds on each side then arrange them on the plate. Serve with rice and a green salad.

Photograph opposite)

Beef with Vegetables in Red Wine Sauce

Preparation time: 30 mins
540 kcal per portion

1 small onion, finely chopped

2 young carrots, halved lengthways

75 ml to 150 ml/3 to 5 fl oz/5 tbsp dry red wine

200 g/7 oz beef fillet steak

a pinch of paprika

freshly ground black pepper

a pinch of dried rosemary

a pinch of dried basil

15 ml/1 tbsp vegetable oil

5 ml/1 tsp butter or margarine

5 ml/1 tsp plain flour

1 Place the onion, carrots and wine in a small saucepan over a medium heat and cook for about 5 minutes, keeping the pan half-covered.
2 While the sauce is cooking, season the beef fillet on both sides with paprika, pepper, rosemary and basil.
3 Heat the oil over a fairly high heat in a frying pan, add steak and fry briskly on both sides until sealed. Reduce the heat and continue to fry the meat until it is cooked to your liking, turning occasionally. Just before the end of the frying time, season to taste with salt. Arrange the steak on a warmed plate and garnish with the carrots.

4 Mix together the butter and flour and whisk it into the sauce over a low heat until the sauce thickens. Cook for 1 minute then spoon the sauce over the steaks. Serve with potato croquettes and pickled red cabbage.

Photograph opposite (top)

Beef with Leek Strips

Preparation time: 15 mins
360 kcal per portion

5 ml/1 tsp butter or margarine

200 g/7 oz beef fillet steak

salt and freshly ground black pepper

a pinch of dried thyme

a pinch of paprika

15 ml/1 tbsp crème fraîche

1 small leek, cut into strips

1 Melt the butter or margarine in a frying pan over a medium heat. Season the beef on both sides with salt, pepper, thyme and paprika.
2 Fry the meat fairly briskly on both sides for about 1 minute, then reduce the heat and fry for a further 3 to 4 minutes, turning 2 or 3 times.
3 Transfer the beef to a warmed plate and keep it warm. Add the leek strips to the pan and cook for about 1 minute over a medium heat. Stir in the crème fraîche and heat through gently without boiling. Arrange the leeks on the plate and serve with boiled potatoes garnished with parsley.

Photograph opposite (bottom)

Lamb Casserole with Vegetables

Preparation time: 1½ hrs
670 kcal per portion

30 ml/2 tbsp oil

150 g/5 oz leg lamb, cubed

1 small onion, chopped

1 clove garlic, crushed

1 small green or red pepper, chopped

1 small courgette, sliced

1 tomato, cut into 8

a pinch of dried thyme

a pinch of paprika

salt and freshly ground black pepper

5 ml/1 tsp butter or margarine

1 Heat the oil in a frying pan, add the meat and fry over a medium to high heat for 2 minutes until sealed, turning frequently. Add the onion, garlic and continue to fry for 3 minutes.
2 Place the courgette and tomato in an ovenproof dish, top with the meat mixture and season with thyme, paprika, salt and pepper. Dot with the butter, cover and bake in a pre-heated oven at 180°C/350°F/gas mark 4 for about 35 minutes. Serve with jacket potatoes.

Photograph opposite (top)

Lamb with Chinese Leaves

Preparation time: 15 mins
650 kcal per portion

200 g/7 oz leg lamb, cubed

a pinch of dried rosemary

salt and white pepper

15 ml/1 tbsp vegetable oil

50 g/12 oz Chinese leaves, cut into strips

1 small onion, finely chopped

½ apple, peeled and chopped 2.5 ml/½ tsp curry powder

1 Season the lamb well with rosemary, salt and pepper.
2 Heat the oil in a frying pan until sizzling. Fry the lamb for 1 minute until sealed then reduce the heat and continue to fry for 5 to 6 minutes. Arrange the lamb on a warmed plate and keep it warm.
3 Add the Chinese leaves, onion and apple pieces to the pan and season with salt, white pepper and curry powder. Saute the vegetables for about 2 minutes only. Arrange the vegetables around the lamb and serve with rye bread with garlic butter (page 21).

Photograph opposite (bottom)

Gourmet Tip
Groundnut oil is a good oil to choose for Chinese cooking, especially stir-frying, as it has a delicate flavour and can be heated to high temperatures.

Lamb Chops with Broccoli Dumplings

Preparation time: 1 hr
850 kcal per portion

---

30 ml/*2 tbsp* butter or margarine

---

5 ml/*1 tsp* plain flour

---

1 egg yolk

---

1 or 2 broccoli florets, finely chopped

---

salt and white pepper

---

a pinch of ground nutmeg

45ml/ *3 tbsp* fresh white breadcrumbs

---

2 lamb chops

---

a pinch of paprika

---

15 ml/*1 tbsp* vegetable oil

---

30 ml/*2 tbsp* freshly grated Parmesan cheese

---

1 Cream the butter or margarine in a warm bowl. Stir in the flour and the egg yolk a little at a time. Gradually add the finely chopped broccoli and season the mixture well with salt, pepper and a little ground nutmeg. Stir in the breadcrumbs and mix together well. Leave to stand for 20 to 30 minutes so that the breadcrumbs can swell.
2 Shape into 2 dumplings and simmer gently in boiling salted water for 12 to 15 minutes.
3 Meanwhile, season the lamb chops on both sides with paprika, salt and pepper.

4 Heat the oil in a frying pan over a medium heat until sizzling. Add chops. Fry briskly on both sides until sealed, then reduce the heat and cook for a further 5 minutes, turning twice.
5 Arrange the dumplings and the chops on a warmed plate. Pour a little melted butter or margarine over the dumplings and sprinkle with the Parmesan.

Gourmet Tip
Roasted sunflower seeds, sprinkled over the chops, add a note of interest.

Chicken Breast with Raisins

Preparation time: 30 mins
660 kcal per portion

5 ml/**1 tsp** vegetable oil
5 ml/**1 tsp** butter or margarine
1 chicken breast
salt and white pepper
150 ml/**¹/₄ pt**/²/₃ cup Madeira or sherry
1 shallot, chopped
10 ml/**2 tsp** raisins
a pinch of dried thyme
a pinch of ground ginger
5 ml/**1 tsp** crème fraîche

1 Heat the oil and butter in a frying pan. Add the chicken and sauté on each side over a medium heat for 3 to 4 minutes. Season with salt and pepper on both sides, and remove from the pan and keep warm.

2 Add the Madeira or sherry to the pan and simmer for 3 minutes, stirring all the time.

3 Add the shallot to the pan with the raisins, thyme and ginger. Simmer for 2 to 3 minutes.

4 Return chicken to the pan and simmer for about 10 minutes until cooked through. Turn the chicken occasionally and baste with the sauce.

5 Finally, stir in the crème fraîche and continue to simmer for 1 minute without allowing the sauce to boil. Curried rice (page 48) and broccoli make good accompaniments.

Photograph (left)
46

Filet of Sole with Prawns

Preparation time: 15 mins
220 kcal per portion

1 large or 2 small sole fillets
juice of 1/2 lemon
salt and white pepper
a pinch of ground cumin
5 ml/**1 tsp** butter or margarine
45 ml/**3 tbsp** dry white wine
30 ml/**2 tbsp** crème fraîche
50 g/2 oz peeled prawns

1 Sprinkle the sole with the lemon juice and season lightly with salt, pepper and cumin.
2 Melt the butter or margarine in a frying pan over a medium heat. Place the sole fillet in the pan and fry on both sides for 2 to 3 minutes, basting from time to time with the liquid.
3 Transfer the fish to a warmed plate and keep it warm.
4 Mix the wine into the pan juices then stir in the crème fraîche. Heat through without allowing the mixture to boil. Remove pan from heat.
5 Add the prawns and stir well, then spoon the prawns and sauce over the sole. Serve with Curried Rice (page 48) and a green salad.

Photograph (right)

Cheese-Stuffed Rissole with Herb Sweetcorn

Preparation time: 30 mins
770 kcal per portion

---

1 small clove garlic, crushed

200 g/**7 oz** minced beef

1 egg

15 ml/**1 tbsp** fresh breadcrumbs

a pinch of dried thyme

salt and freshly ground black pepper

25 g/**1 oz** Edam cheese

15 ml/**1 tbsp** vegetable oil

10 ml/**2 tsp** chopped fresh parsley

100 g/**4 oz** canned sweetcorn

---

1 Mix together the garlic, beef, egg, breadcrumbs, thyme, salt and pepper. If the mixture is too wet, add as many more breadcrumbs as is necessary to bind the mixture well together. Shape into 1 or 2 rissoles, moulding them round a piece of cheese.
2 Heat the oil in a frying pan over a medium heat and briskly fry the rissoles on both sides. Reduce the heat and continue to fry for 4 minutes on each side. Transfer to a warmed plate and keep warm.

3 Quickly warm up the herbs and the sweetcorn in the same frying pan and serve with the rissoles.

Photograph opposite (top)

Gourmet Tip
Instead of Edam cheese, plain or smoked tofu can be used as a filling. The rissoles are also delicious eaten cold.

Rissole with Capers and Curried Rice

Preparation time: 30 mins
620 kcal per portion

---

50 g/**2 oz** long-grain rice

5 ml/**1 tsp** turmeric

5 ml/**1 tsp** curry powder

a pinch of salt

5 ml/**1 tsp** capers, chopped

1 small pickled gherkin, chopped

200 g/**7 oz** minced beef

2.5 ml/$^1/_2$ **tsp** green peppercorns

2.5 ml/$^1/_2$ **tsp** paprika

freshly ground black pepper

a pinch of dried rosemary

a pinch of dried thyme

a pinch of dried basil

30 ml/**2 tbsp** vegetable oil

15 ml/**1 tbsp** chopped fresh parsley

---

1 Boil the rice in double its volume of water with the turmeric, curry powder and salt for about 12 to 15 minutes.
2 Mix together the capers, gherkin, beef, peppercorns, paprika and herbs. Shape into a round rissole.
3 Heat the oil in a frying pan until sizzling. Add the rissole and fry briskly on both sides for about 1 minute. Reduce the heat and continue to fry for a further 6 minutes, turning twice.
4 Drain the rice and serve with rissole, sprinkled with parsley.

Photograph opposite (bottom)

Gourmet Tip
Instead of capers, half a small pickled pepper, finely chopped, can be added to the minced meat mixture. Sauté potatoes can be substituted for curried rice.

Cheese and Ham Macaroni with Broccoli

Preparation time: 30 mins
1100 kcal per portion

100 g/4 oz macaroni

salt

10 ml/2 tsp butter or margarine

45 ml/3 tbsp single cream

1 egg

white pepper

a pinch of dried marjoram

a pinch of dried thyme

a pinch of ground nutmeg

2 small slices cooked ham, cubed

50 g/2 oz Emmental cheese, grated

150 g/5 oz broccoli florets

1 Cook the macaroni in boiling lightly salted water until just tender, *al dente*. Drain and put aside.
2 Grease an ovenproof dish with the butter or margarine.
3 Whisk the cream and egg and season with white pepper, marjoram, thyme and nutmeg.
6 Place the macaroni in the prepared dish and sprinkle ham cubes over the top. Pour over the egg mixture and sprinkle with the Emmental cheese. Bake in a preheated oven at 200°C/400°F/gas mark 6 for 20 minutes until the cheese has melted and the top is a crusty golden brown.

5 Meanwhile, cook the broccoli in a little boiling salted water for about 5 minutes until just tender. Season to taste with salt, pepper and marjoram and serve with the macaroni.

Photograph opposite (top)

> **Gourmet Tip**
> You can add the precooked broccoli to the dish if you prefer.

Stuffed Courgette Boats

Preparation time: 1¼ hrs
870 kcal per portion

1 large courgette, halved lengthways

salt and white pepper

a pinch of dried rosemary

10 ml/2 tsp vegetable oil

200 g/7 oz minced pork

1 clove garlic, sliced

1 Hollow out the centre of the courgette with a spoon. Season the halves with salt, pepper and rosemary. Sprinkle with oil.
2 Fill up the hollowed out courgette halves with the minced meat and press the garlic slices into the meat.
3 Place the courgette halves into an ovenproof dish and cook in a preheated oven at 200°C/400°F/gas mark 6 for 40 to 50 minutes, turning off the oven after 30 minutes. Serve with your favourite vegetables.

Photograph opposite (bottom)

Desserts

Some people believe that the dessert is the best part of a meal. It will certainly be hard to resist some of the following tempting sweets.

Vanilla Ice Cream with Marzipan Dates, page 54

Vanilla Ice Cream with Marzipan Dates

Preparation time: 15 mins
580 kcal per portion

---

6 large dried dates

50 g/2 oz marzipan

100 g/4 oz vanilla ice cream

50 g/2 oz plain chocolate

30 ml/2 tbsp golden syrup

---

1 Cut the dates open lengthways and remove the stones. Fill the insides with marzipan.
2 Scoop the ice cream on to a flat plate. Arrange the dates round the ice cream.
3 Gently melt the chocolate with the syrup. As soon as the chocolate has melted, pour it over the ice cream.

Photograph page 52

Gourmet Tip
Instead of dates, take 12 walnut halves and sandwich them together with marzipan.

Grapes with Brandy Coating

Preparation time: 15 mins
200 kcal per portion

---

100 g/4 oz grapes

10 ml/2 tsp honey

10 ml/2 tsp brandy

10 ml/2 tsp icing sugar

---

1 Divide the grapes into clusters.
2 Place a small dish in a bowl of hot water and put in the honey. As soon as the honey has melted stir in the brandy. Put the icing sugar in a little dish.
3 Hold the grapes by the stalk and dip them in the honey and brandy mixture. Sprinkle with the icing sugar and serve immediately.

Photograph opposite (top)

Gourmet Tip
For a more crunchy effect, use caster instead of icing sugar.

Figs in Wine Sauce

Preparation time: 25 mins
plus soaking
250 kcal per portion

---

50 g/2 oz dried figs

1 clove

150 ml/¹/₄ pt/²/₃ cup sweet white wine

5 ml/1 tsp rum

a pinch of ground ginger

---

1 Soak figs and clove overnight in the wine so that they soften and swell.
2 Simmer the figs in the wine for about 10 minutes or until soft.
3 Remove the figs and the clove from the pan and boil the wine for about 10 minutes to reduce it. Just before the end of the cooking time, add the rum and the ginger.
4 Arrange the figs in a small dessert dish and pour over the wine sauce.

Photograph opposite (bottom)

Fruity Fromage Frais

Preparation time: 15 mins
510 kcal per portion

---

150 g/5 oz fromage frais

30 ml/2 tbsp whipping cream

1 small banana

juice of 1/2 lemon

1 ripe peach, peeled, halved and stoned

a pinch of chopped fresh mint

10 ml/2 tsp honey

---

1 Mix the fromage frais with the cream. Mash the banana with the lemon juice. Cut one peach half into cubes and the other into segments.
2 Add the bananas, peach cubes, mint and honey to the cream, stirring gently until well mixed.
3 Transfer to a dish and decorate with peach segments.

Photograph opposite (top right)

Apple Snow with Raisins

Preparation time: 20 mins plus chilling
200 kcal per portion

---

1 cooking apple, peeled, cored and cubed

10 ml/2 tsp lemon juice

10 ml/2 tsp apricot jam

10 ml/2 tsp raisins

1 egg white

Grated chocolate, crushed flake bar or chocolate vermicelli

---

1 Place the apple, lemon juice, jam and raisins in a small saucepan. Cover and cook over a low heat until soft, adding a little water if necessary to prevent the apple from burning.
2 Break the mixture down with a fork and beat with a whisk until smooth. Chill the purée in the refrigerator for 40 to 50 minutes.
3 Beat the egg white until stiff and carefully fold into the apple mixture. Transfer to a dish and sprinkle with chocolate.

Photograph opposite (centre left)

Wine Cream with Saffron

Preparation time: 15 mins plus standing
500 kcal per portion

---

45 ml/3 tbsp dry white wine

a pinch of saffron powder

a pinch of ground ginger

2.5 ml/1/2 tsp grated lemon rind

15 ml/1 tbsp ground almonds

15 ml/1 tbsp honey

120 ml/4 fl oz/1/2 cup double cream

a few whole blanched almonds

---

1 Mix together the wine, saffron, ginger, lemon rind and ground almonds and leave the mixture to stand for about 2 hours.
2 Add honey and cream and beat until thick and creamy.
3 Transfer to dessert dish and garnish with the almonds.

Photograph opposite (bottom)

Spicy Pancakes

Preparation time: 25 mins
600 kcal per portion

---

15 ml/*1 tbsp* butter or
margarine

50 g/ 2 oz plain flour

a pinch of saffron powder

a pinch of ground ginger

5 ml/ 1 tsp soft brown sugar

a pinch of salt

1 egg

150 ml/*¹/₄ pt/²/₃ cup* milk

butter or margarine for
frying

a little honey, jam or apple
purée for spreading

5 ml/*1 tsp* icing sugar

---

1 Melt the butter or mar-
garine and leave to cool
slightly.
2 Sieve the flour into a
bowl and mix in the saf-
fron, ginger, brown sugar
and a little salt.
3 Add the egg and milk a
little at a time, beating
continuously until the batter is smooth and creamy.
Finally, stir in the melted
butter.
4 Heat a frying pan over a
medium heat and brush
the base with a little soft
butter or margarine using
a pastry brush or twist of
greaseproof paper.
5 Pour just enough batter
into the pan to cover the
base and fry until cooked
on one side. Flip over and
cook the other side.
Transfer to a warmed
plate and keep the pan-
cake warm while you fry
the remainder.

6 Spread the pancakes
with honey, jam or apple
purée and roll up. Sprinkle
with icing sugar.

Gourmet Tip
To serve the
pancakes with
chocolate sauce,
slowly warm
30 ml/2 tbsp of
chocolate sauce with
a dash or two of
Cointreau. Add a
little chopped
preserved ginger
and spoon over the
pancakes.

Blackberry Gratin

Preparation time: 1 hr
660 kcal per portion

---

50 g/*2 oz* blackberries

15 ml/*1 tbsp* caster sugar

5 ml/*1 tsp* raspberry syrup
or Kirsch liqueur

1 egg

120 ml/*4 fl oz*/*¹/₂ cup*
whipping cream

15 ml/*1 tbsp* softened butter
or margarine

15 ml/*1 tbsp* icing sugar

---

1 Place the blackberries
in a greased gratin dish
and sprinkle with half the
sugar and the syrup or
Kirsch.
2 Beat the egg with the
remaining sugar and the
cream. Spoon over the
blackberries and top with
flakes of butter.
3 Bake in a preheated
oven at 180°C/350°F/gas
mark 4 for 10 minutes,
sprinkle with icing sugar
and continue to cook for a
further 15 minutes. Serve
hot.

*Photograph opposite
(top)*

Raspberries with Almond Cream

Preparation time: 30 mins
400 kcal per portion

---

50 g/*2 oz* fresh raspberries

1 egg, separated

15 ml/*1 tbsp* icing sugar

25 g/*1 oz* ground almonds

15 ml/*1 tbsp* whipping
cream

5 ml/*1 tsp* butter or
margarine

icing sugar for sprinkling

---

1 Beat the egg yolk with
the icing sugar until
creamy. Fold in the
ground almonds.
2 Beat the egg white until
stiff and carefully fold it
into the almond mixture.
3 Grease an ovenproof
dish with the butter or
margarine. Put in half the
almond mixture, sprinkle
with raspberries then coat
with the remaining al-
mond mixture.
4 Bake in a preheated
oven at 180°C/350°F/gas
mark 4 for 10 to 15 min-
utes until puffy. Sprinkle
with icing sugar and serve
warm.

*Photograph opposite
(centre)*

Swiss Chocolate

Preparation time: 30 mins
830 kcal per portion

---

15 ml/*1 tbsp* butter or
margarine

1 egg yolk

30 ml/*2 tbsp* caster sugar

25 g/*1 oz* ground almonds

15 ml/*1 tbsp* grated rye
bread

50 g/*2 oz* plain chocolate

1 egg white

a pinch of salt

butter or margarine for
greasing

fresh breadcrumbs for
sprinkling

---

1 Melt the butter or mar-
garine and leave it to cool
slightly. Pre-heat oven to
180°C/350°F/gas mark 4.
2 Beat the egg yolk with
the sugar until thick and
creamy. Mix in the al-
monds, rye bread and
melted butter or
margarine.
3 Melt the chocolate with
10 ml/2 tsp of water. Stir it
into the egg mixture.
4 Beat the egg white with
the salt until stiff and fold
into the chocolate mix-
ture, a spoonful at a time.
5 Grease a small soufflé
dish with butter or mar-
garine and sprinkle with
breadcrumbs. Spoon in
the chocolate mixture and
bake in a preheated oven
at 180°C/350°F/gas mark
4 for 20 minutes without
opening the oven door.
Serve straight away.

*Photograph opposite
(bottom)*

Apple Tart

Preparation time: 30 mins
290 kcal per portion

| 1 apple, peeled and cored |
| 90 ml/**6 tbsp** red wine |
| 10 ml/**2 tsp** caster sugar |
| 1 flan tartlet case |
| 15 ml/**1 tbsp** natural yoghurt |
| 2.5 ml/**1/2 tsp** cornflour |
| 15 ml/**1 tbsp** cashew nuts |

1 Place the apple in a small saucepan with the wine and half the sugar, cover and cook over a low heat for about 9 minutes until the apple has softened. Remove the apple from the wine and cut into segments.

2 Fill the tartlet case with the yoghurt then top with the apple slices.
3 Stir the cornflour into the wine, bring to the boil and cook, stirring, for a few minutes until thickened. Spoon over the apples and sprinkle with the cashew nuts.

> **Gourmet Tip**
> You can use a pear instead of an apple and sprinkle the dish with chopped pistachios.

GOURMET COOKSHELF...

...Pretty little books that make excellent "thank you" gifts. Or better still for your own Life Style uplift.

GOURMET COOKSHELF...

...For the kind of cook who seriously enjoys eating good food, but doesn't enjoy spending days in the kitchen to prepare.

GOURMET COOKSHELF...

...Books for cooks to collect, that will produce that uplifting recipe whenever you feel like something enticing.

- ◆ Regional Chinese Specialities
- ◆ Wok Specialities
- ◆ Cooking for One or Two
- ◆ Regional Italian Specialities
- ◆ Grills and Barbeques
- ◆ Spaghetti, Tagliatelle Etc...

- ◆ Fondues
- ◆ Pasta
- ◆ Desserts
- ◆ Finger Food
- ◆ Fish
- ◆ Sauces

and yet more to come — be sure of that!

For details write to:
W. Foulsham, Yeovil Road, Slough, Berkshire SL1 4JH.

Index of Recipes

foulsham
Yeovil Road, Slough, Berkshire, SL1 4JH

ISBN 0-572-01766-9

This English language edition copyright
© 1992 W. Foulsham & Co. Ltd
Originally published by Falken-Verlag,
GmbH, Nidernhausen TS, Germany
Photographs copyright © Falken-Verlag

Printed in Portugal